The Disappearing SISTER

ELIZABETH CUMMINGS

For Families in Need Everywhere
And for the survivors of ED - the bravest of them all.

I have a big sister.

She is really clever and pretty.
I wish I could do what she can do.
She is my hero.

But there is this thing with my sister.
She has started to disappear.
It's weird...

...sometimes even her smile
disappears and her voice changes.
It's not her.

She can make other things disappear too.
Like her breakfast, like her lunch...

...like her dinner.
I have to promise not to tell.

Sometimes she lets me in her room, and sometimes I go into her room when she doesn't know it, and I just watch her.....

...I look at her really hard and I think she isn't really there, not really, where is she?

Sometimes she can't see me either. Is it just me who sees she isn't really there?

Mum says she is just a teenager.
I say she is **NOT** my sister.

Dad says she's busy studying. I say how can she when she is too sick to eat?

My friend Jennie understands.
She sees what I see.

"You must tell your mum," says Jennie.
"How can I? I don't want my sister to be
mad I promised not to tell?"

"Well I didn't promise," says Jennie and she tells my mum.

What have we done?
My sister is so angry.
Mum says it is not my sister
being angry — it's the illness

We go to the doctor. All together. Me, Mum, Dad and my disappearing sister.

The doctor talks for ages.... It makes my sister cry, it makes mum cry, it makes dad cry....it makes me cry...

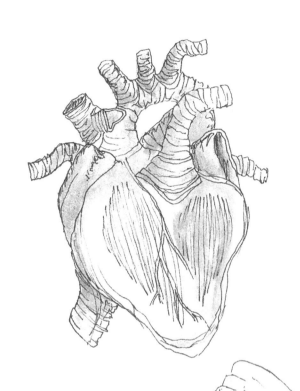

The doctor says her heart is wasting away as she does not have enough **NUTRITION** for her body.

He says that her heart is disappearing - she is disappearing from the inside too....

The doctors says she
needs **TOTAL** rest.
The nurse says she
needs to eat.

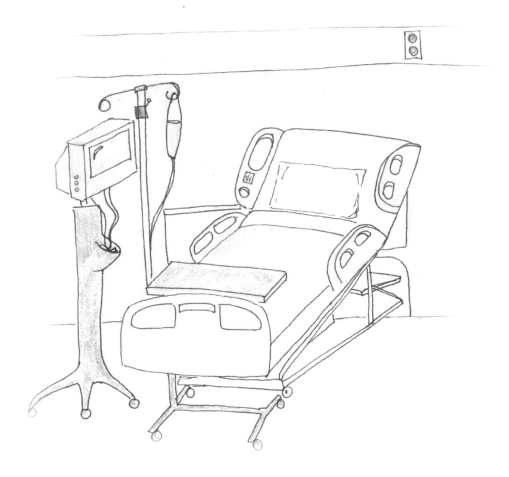

Mum says she needs to eat much more than anyone else in the family and we must all help, but first a special holiday for my sister.

Dad says that tube feeds her when she sleeps — she needs more energy.
Dad looks sooo sad. But then he smiles and tells me I am a brave girl.

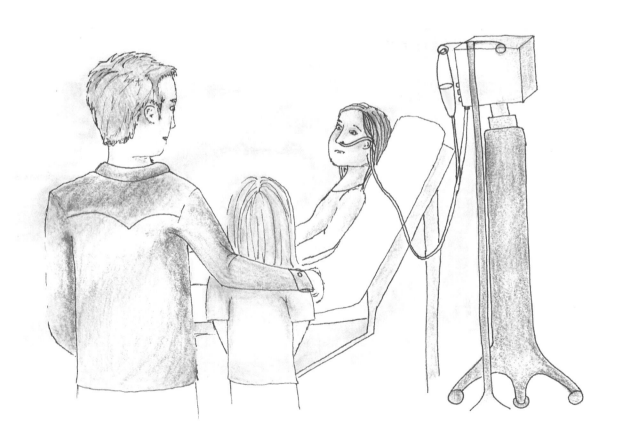

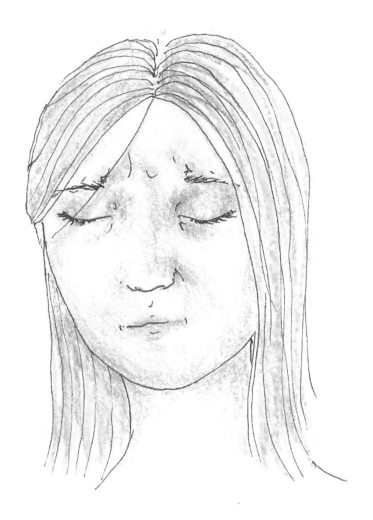

It is my sister who is brave...

I

just

want

to

run

away...

My sister is almost
totally disappeared now
I cannot see her
when she is lying down.

I cannot see her
when she is standing up
I cannot see her
when she eats.

Why is she not better?
When will she get better?
How long will it take?
Why can't she see
she is disappearing?

Sometimes I can not remember
what my real sister was like.

Other days are OK.
Now my sister wants to stop disappearing
but it is a hard thing to do.

Sometimes she thinks she can't do it.
Sometimes mum thinks she can't do it.
Sometimes dad thinks she can't do it.
Can she do it?
It's so hard for her, so very, very hard.

She has to do it — I need my sister back.
Please come back, I love you, I can help you.

We can do this together.
She can come back.

It might take a long time...
...but...

...I know she can do this!

About the Author

Elizabeth Cummings studied Psychology and Business Studies at Edinburgh university before becoming a primary school teacher. She has travelled and lived overseas most of her adult life and now lives with her husband and two daughters in Coogee in Sydney.

Throughout her working life, and in recent times in her personal life, Elizabeth has worked and supported families living with the trauma of health issues including those associated with eating disorders. Currently there is little literature geared towards the direct empowerment of siblings of ED sufferers and this book is aimed at providing a platform by which discussion may be started in a guided environment to help young children understand the nature of an ED illness. As well as this Elizabeth hopes that this story might help families identify how the whole family is needed to help their loved one on the long road of their recovery to full health.

Lightning Source UK Ltd.
Milton Keynes UK
UKOW07f0701120515

251324UK00002BA/7/P